Love Bites

Dearest
Hi Canada
Vancouver Jericho
Beach!

VANNDANA VAADERA

Tons of love
Dr. Vanndana Vaadera
9/9/2024!

notionpress.com

INDIA · SINGAPORE · MALAYSIA

Notion Press

No. 8, 3rd Cross Street
CIT Colony, Mylapore
Chennai, Tamil Nadu – 600004

First Published by Notion Press 2021
Copyright © Vanndana Vaadera 2021
All Rights Reserved.

ISBN 978-1-63669-610-2

This book has been published with all efforts taken to make the material error-free after the consent of the author. However, the author and the publisher do not assume and hereby disclaim any liability to any party for any loss, damage, or disruption caused by errors or omissions, whether such errors or omissions result from negligence, accident, or any other cause.

While every effort has been made to avoid any mistake or omission, this publication is being sold on the condition and understanding that neither the author nor the publishers or printers would be liable in any manner to any person by reason of any mistake or omission in this publication or for any action taken or omitted to be taken or advice rendered or accepted on the basis of this work. For any defect in printing or binding the publishers will be liable only to replace the defective copy by another copy of this work then available.

In this book, each chapter has a part of my life—a tiny part of me!

Contents

Prologue 7

1. Introduction: My Inspiring Story 9
2. Arrested On Holi! 23
3. Berlin: An Affair to Remember 31
4. A Serial Dater, a Man on the Menu - Next, Please! 39
5. A Brush with Lesbianism!!!!! 43
6. Jane Austen Revisited - A Fairytale Romance 49
7. "HUSSY"… TOE… PHASI!!!!
   [If She laughs she is trapped] 59
8. Miss Misfortune - Part 2 63
9. Slavery, Thy Name is Woman? is
   Your Guy a "BI"? – Reflect, Woman 67
10. Mystic Magical Fairyland: Glastonbury 73

11. The Cat's Tryst With The Cat 91
12. Arjun On My Mind, Arjun In My Heart! 95

Epilogue 99

Prologue

I had always wanted to author a book. I have been writing articles on my life's experiences for my blog. Somehow it seemed right to compile them all in one place for the world to read.

My sanskaras include courage, freedom, love, friendship, bluntness, spirituality, humour, fun and adventure. Till date I seek all these, in every task I undertake. They reflect in my style of writing and are revealed in the stories that follow in this book.

I have always lived life with positive affirmations. I am a dreamer and my positive frame of mind, has helped me triumph my dreams and make them my reality. I solicit the power of manifestations in everything I do.

I echo the quote of Lord Buddha, "You think you become"!

CHAPTER

01

Introduction: My Inspiring Story

I am Vanndana Vaadera, a TV, radio, and live stage anchor. Also, a motivational speaker, speech coach, and a life transformation coach. I have been in the industry for the last 26 years. Having worked with top conglomerates, Hollywood and Bollywood stars, and with several prime ministers of various countries, I have trained innumerable CEOs as iconic speakers and transformed them internally, with my programs. Yet, today, I feel humbled that I can still call myself a learner, a student of life.

My parents are from a modest middle-class background. My father is a highly qualified, retired army officer, and my late mother, was an exceedingly educated English language and literature teacher.

While growing up, we did not have the luxuries, that kids have today.

But my parents made sure I got the best education and upbringing. Although, observing my status today, people feel that my life was a cakewalk! No, my dear friends, the odyssey was certainly not a bed of roses!

So, here I present my journey of life. For all you know, it may inspire someone out there, to wake up, take action, and surge ahead to become a conquistador. And if it does, I would have lived my life's purpose.

* * *

While spinning tales of my childhood, the laughter, the pain, and the joy of life, I relate one incident that had an immense impact on my brain and subconscious mind. This defining moment, down the years, carved out a whole new, empowered me!

The story commences on the 1st of January 1974. I am playing in the beautiful garden of a house in Amritsar, Punjab, India, with my siblings—eldest brother Sharad, sister Poonam, aged 5; I am a tender Three-year-old toddler! It's even a greater surprise that I recall this significant episode, so vividly.

We children are excited as we are going to catch the train to Lucknow, to spend our vacations with our maternal grandparents.

There is a rumble of the gravel in the pathway outside the gate. An army truck, what we call a one-ton vehicle, stops midway. My sister has an idea. She had always been the most intelligent one to conjure plans.

She suggests that we three siblings have a race to see who arrives and climbs the back of the vehicle first! So, we form a line, with her on my extreme left, myself in the middle, and my brother on the extreme right, clasping each other's hands.

She counts, one, two, three, GO! Before my brother could react, as he pulls me back toward him, she yanks her hand out of my tiny fingers and sprints ahead, at full speed.

She arrives at the truck, grabs the heavy chain, and heaves herself up, one leg on board and the other dangling in midair, looking back triumphantly at us, with a look that says, "See, I won!"

Unfortunately, the driver, who does not know what is happening behind, puts the truck in reverse gear. With a jolt, Poonam lurched onto the graveled pathway in a second. Before she could pick herself up, the wheel of the heavy one-ton truck passes over her head!! I am just staring! Silent! Baffled! Puzzled! Scared!

I am dazed, never having seen death before.

I walk baby steps. I sit down beside her limp body, shaking her, nudging her gently, trying to wake her up, "wakeup Poony, wakeup!"

Mummy runs out with Papa, stops dead in her track, staring at the gruesome sight, trying to take in the situation, not being able to comprehend what lay in front of them. Complete shock, silence, disbelief.

Today when I reflect back, I can very well imagine what was running through her head. A mix of emotions. that were choking up her brain—pain, hurt, repentance, guilt!

In a state of trance, not able to understand the facts, a shattered father carries the body inside.

The next few days that pass by, the trauma is so great that Mummy has completely forgotten that she has another child, craving her attention, whose world revolves around her mother! Mamma does not hug or cuddle me anymore, constantly grieving for my sister, whom she had to burn with her own hands. I am confused, trying to grab her attention, but to no avail.

The kind neighbors, in the city of Amritsar, take me in, nurture me, feed me, while I only crave my mother's love. I am not able to understand what I did wrong. Why am I being punished? What happened was my fault? Why can't I play with my sister anymore? Where is she? Why does no one want me?

Then, another unfortunate thing happens. The shock of the scene witnessed by me, and my mother not caring for me, has such an immense impact on my mind that I am discovered, unconscious, convulsing with epileptic seizures. I start getting attacks whilst sleeping. Mouth frothing, biting my tongue, bleeding, waking up suddenly, staring into the darkness. A frightened, distraught, hysterical child!

Days turn into months, Mummy neither cries nor reacts. My state, deteriorating, and so was her's.

Three months later, with umpteen visits to doctors and healers, my mother is made to realize by well-wishers, that she will lose another child if she does not come to terms with reality. One daughter has gone, one is still there. Embrace her, love her.

Then commenced the story of even greater love, strength, and transformation. The unconditional devotion and guardianship of the lady who became my pillar of strength.

She instilled in me the belief that I was the best thing that ever happened to her. I was a champion, a powerful bundle of energy and vigor, who could never ever be vanquished.

She instilled in me the belief that every task I put my heart into, I would emerge triumphant, and under no circumstance would she ever lose me.

She brought me up so beautifully that I grew up to be this ironwoman, unstoppable me.

With proper treatment, love, and nurturing, I healed fast. But the story of my innumerable struggles does not end here...

Life has a wicked sense of humor; fast forward to 1993.

I rebelled with my family, fell in love, and got married to my college senior, thinking love would conquer all. The courtship period is a fairytale. Everything seems rosy and wistful before marriage! So, what if our family backgrounds don't match? So, what if no one, except him, in his family had cleared the 10th grade? Did it matter that they lived in just one room?

Alas, a very bad decision! He was jobless, so I took employment as a fashion design teacher and got a meagre salary of 4000 rupees, which my mother in law would deposit in our joint account, of which she was the only signing authority.

I got trampled, beaten black and blue, every second day on the pretext that "Vanndana argues too much." It would shock you to know, that I was attacked even on the 6th day of marriage. I would run away from their house and hide behind the Durga statue in the Mandir nearby, for three days at a stretch! The temple priest would hand me fruits and prasad. No one would bother to come looking for me.

For 11 months, I suffered torture, not breathing a word to my parents. His mother finally cast me out of the house. I scouted a tiny one-room accommodation and stayed there. He displayed to the world, that he was leaving his house to live with me. But he never turned up after the first day. I had made him a copy of my house keys. Finally, on the 31st of December 1994, he stole all my jewelry and absconded, while I was at my institute, teaching.

That was the day my mother brought me back home. My father was reluctant to take me back, but Mamma, the powerful woman she was, put her foot down, "If Vanndana leaves, I go with her! I am getting accommodation in the Army Public School where I am an English Literature Language teacher, we mother-daughter will be very happy there!" That was enough for Papa to take me back!

* * *

She rebuilt the faith I had lost in life, harnessed the strength in me which had vanished completely. I had started believing I was not worthy of love and deserved all the abuse because I was a woman. She encouraged me to start my recordings, do theater, television, she got my professional portfolio done, to make me fathom, that I was dazzling, stunning, inside and outside, so that my confidence would come bouncing back!

It seemed God was hell-bent upon testing our lives... Another woe strikes. Even before my divorce could come through, my mother passed away... I was shattered, even thought of committing suicide, as I felt responsible for her death. Her body came back from Shimla wrapped in gauze, lying on ice slabs in a three-ton Shaktiman vehicle. That unnerving vision does not leave my consciousness to date!

I bathed her, decked her up like a newlywed bride, with a heavy bleeding heart, and bid her adieu. I could have just given up my hold on life, as I felt I had nothing left to live for. My pillar of strength was gone.

But slowly, I drew strength from inside me. I recollected the undying faith my mother had in me. I recalled her words, which had become my 'imprints' since childhood, "You are a winner, the most intelligent one in the family. You will be triumphant always." I kept reminding myself of my codes, my imprints and vaulted back to life. I rejoined the institute where I taught, started my music dubbings with various renowned singers, like Daler Mehndi, started giving auditions for TV serials, getting back to my acting days, approaching event companies, pitching myself as an anchor, singer, and speaker. I was hell-bent upon putting all that I had absorbed from my diva mom to practice, and emerge triumphantly.

I had just a one-point focus: I have to make her dreams my reality, coz I am *her* champion!

* * *

Remember, failure is not tumbling down; it's refusing to get up and try again. Rebuild your castle of dreams, and make those dreams a reality! This is just one of the painful stories of my life. Maybe in the future, I will recount more as life unfolds further in its sweet and sour topsy-turvy ways.

So, I stand in front of all of you, successful against odds, performing luminously, with my own house in Mumbai and two floors in Delhi in a posh locality. I have earned name, fame, worked with the best in the industry, and now it's time to give back to the world from my experiences, lessons, knowledge, and wisdom which is evolving even as I pen these pages.

Col K.L. Vadehra and Late Mrs Meera Vadehra

Col K.L. Vadehra[Retd], Vanndana Vaadera, Sharad Vadehra and Late Mrs Meera Vadehra

Vanndana Vaadera

John Travolta and Vanndana Vaadera

Col K.L. Vadehra[Retd] and Vanndana Vaadera

Smt. Rajeshwari Tandon
Social Secretary to PM

N.I (10) 85-PMPI

प्रधान मंत्री कार्यालय
नई दिल्ली - 110011
PRIME MINISTER'S OFFICE
NEW DELHI - 110011

July 26, 1985

3 0 JUL 1985

Dear Vandana,

    The Prime Minister Shri Rajiv Gandhi thanks you for your letter of July 20 and the poem which you have shared with him. He sends his good wishes for your studies and a future as lovely as the rainbow you described.

    I am sure you will appreciate the Prime Minister's difficulty in meeting the innumerable young people who have made similar requests, specially due to his preoccupations.

Yours sincerely,

(Rajeshwari Tandon)

Miss Vandana Vadehra
D/o Maj. K.L. Vadehra
B-2/47C DDA Flats
Lawrence Road
Delhi 110035

Letter from the late PM Shri Rajeev Gandhi

CHAPTER

02

Arrested On Holi!

March 18, 2009, at 1:32 AM
NOW WHO WANTS UNLIMITED SEX ON HOLI???
AND WANTS TO GET ARRESTED WHILE DOING IT!!:)??

Ahaan!! Having grabbed your attention, I will come straight to the main reason why this write-up was given birth! Although, I must confess that the prologue has little to do with the contents that follow…

It has come to my knowledge that there are many Homo sapiens who have been perpetually tagged with misfortune and unforeseen circumstances. They are 24x7 the victims of weird happenings, not initiated by them. Basically, they are slaves to Miss Calamity and ought to be labeled Red, Hot, and Dangerous explosives that may go "Kaboom" any moment!

Now for all those who are totally nonplussed as to where is this leading, allow me to put your doubts to rest. We are describing "me", a clumsy species that eternally has trouble tailing her and seems to become the object of mirth, hence providing constant entertainment to people, so frequently, that she could qualify as Mr. Bean's sibling.

One of the innumerable hilarious episodes, which at the moment of the mishap seemed far from it, is the Holi havoc. Having lost the entire set of my room keys, I needed to have my bedroom handle lock changed, which was instantly done by a carpenter working in the apartment below. The morning after, the "unholy-Holi" morning, I awaken to the fact that I am not able to open the door as the handle had been set free! Still hungover by lack of sleep and an unfocused mind, with all my might, my will, and my determination, I try to yield as much pressure on the handle as possible. Finally, the poor unassuming metal yanks and snaps from its spring, into a sweaty, clammy palm, blushing with gnawingly painful blisters!!

For a moment, I felt the strength of Mike Tyson flowing through my veins, but the euphoria was short-lived! Woe of woes, the 24-hour help lady was on a festive vacation. With both my mobile phones getting charged in the study, my telephone directory being marked absent from the room, a dead wi-fi connection as my laptop had been mercilessly damaged by my inadequacy with techno gizmos, where did I stand??? ? I had the main gate's giant key with me inside the room. Ah, an obsolete non-functional landline, lying in a corner of the room. To get it working and alive again, it had to be charged. Eureka!! I remembered my dad's number. Engaged!! He seemed to be preoccupied, chatting up with uncles his age, probably making plans to congregate in the colony park to enjoy a leisurely, blissfully colorful Holi!

Fortunately, my room has a window that opens into the back ally. I catch a glimpse of the servant's kids and some grownups smothering each other with auspicious Gulal.

"Help!"

I bellow. "I am under house arrest by my own will and, not to mention, my foolhardiness. Please take the keys and rescue me!" They gaze at me as though I am pouring Latin, French, and Greek into their benevolent ears. "Fool!" I mentally reprimand myself; "It's Hindi that works wonders in such situations."

After having thrown my keys across, I was knocked into the realization, that even if they unlocked the main gate, there was the iron bolt and the wooden door to combat with. Trials never end. They say that the penultimate test is always in hot waters [or maybe something like that]. I need such adventurous and audacious situations to get my idle brain functioning. Then the idea struck me like a bolt of lightning: when in trouble, dial 100, and indeed that was the brainwave of the holy day, I mean the *holi*-day.

"Police beat room!" cooed a voice, which sounded like music to my ears. Having explained my situation, all I had to do was wait. Taking advantage of the time at hand, I showered and got dressed to play the festive Holi with friends. Although I must add, it was not at all tasteful witnessing eight men clothed in police uniform, crackling in a heavy Haryanvi accent, breaking the main door, and raiding my entire house. Yet, at that moment I could comprehend the significance of the term "freedom."

With the newly acquired autonomy, I was all set to enjoy it to the hilt, armed with new confidence, a new life, a new meaning!! Ouch! Okay, I know, I know, it's getting way out of hand. So, we come to the end of episode one of the first day series. Episode two of the same day to follow soon! All's well that ends well. May we all stay blessed!

Amit Talwar, Preeti Singh and Vanndana Vaadera

Meenakshi Dutt, Amit Talwar, Preeti Singh and Vanndana Vaadera

Dolly, Vanndana Vaadera, Rajeev Jain and Shweta Rai

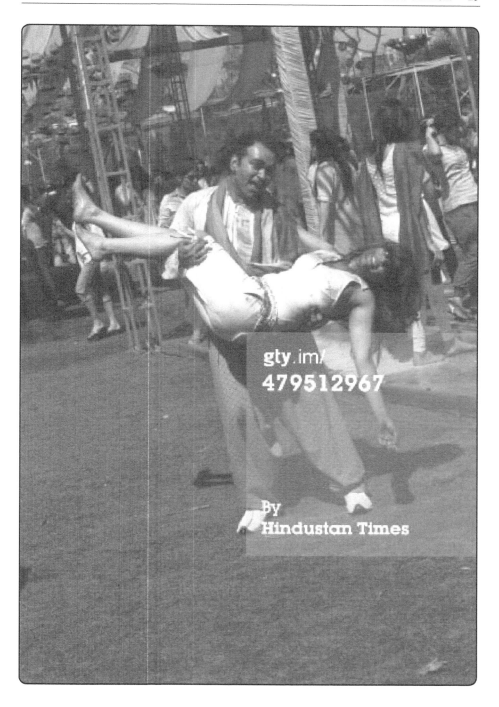

Amit Talwar and Vanndana Vaadera

CHAPTER

03

Berlin: An Affair to Remember

September 17, 2008 at 1:03 PM
BERLIN BONANZA!!

The chronicles of a lady bitten by the travel bug are vast, full of adventure, excitement, and mystery. A yearning to explore the world takes her to the realms of the world which echo sometimes with the epics of ancient history, romance, with classic exquisite architecture, pure heritage, culture, and, at other times, simply virgin exotic beauty! What better place to start the travelogue than the bountiful enigma of Europe, and within Europe, the capital of Germany,Berlin.

Berlin is one such city that holds a heady cocktail of all these, shaken and stirred into a mélange of memories that one carries back home. With my traveling head firmly on, scouting the capital of Germany was indeed an exhilarating experience. Well, I am not as lavishly spoiled as I am overindulged, thanks to my patrons. So, having checked in at the Ritz Carlton, I was all charged up to party, explore the city, and paint the town red! No amount of jet lag could bind me to my comfortable king-sized double bed.

My first destination was a lavish reception party thrown at the Charlottenburg Palace, in West Berlin. The mammoth château hosts decorative arts, paintings, Prussian architecture, palatial botanical gardens—a perfect setting to relax my aching joints in vials of pinot noir and medium-bodied sweet Italian merlot wine and sway a soft waltz to the cello and violins, penetrating the intoxicated night! I strongly feel that men outside India notice you more, are excessively romantic, approach you, and you stand a better chance of discovering your soulmate, if such a thing exists!

I will not be delving into the details of the conference or my public musical performances and simply stick to the travel part, so you don't have to question the nature of my expedition.

The next day was time for exploring the city, which was once East Berlin and had been completely destroyed in the air raids in 1943, and what could be more exciting than to jump into a Trabant safari. Incidentally, Trabants are obsolete cars, which were built in the 1950s in East Germany and are quaint replicas of the old station wagon, except that they have a weird two-stroke engine under the bonnet! It was definitely a tight squeeze, but the ride was worth the trouble.

The caravan of five cars set out on a guided tour, unfolding each building en route.

They say when you are in love with a city, you flirt with everything that comes your way, the buildings, the cars, the bystander, and everything flirts right back with you!

Our archaic, old-fashioned cars drew enough attention, as mirth amongst the onlookers was audible. We became specimens to be clicked by spectators, rather than the other way around.

As the caravan proceeded, we passed by several important buildings, the main one being the theater for cabaret reviews, now that sounded very interesting [should go and shake a booty there!]. Then came the remnants of the Berlin Wall, laid in a line of bricks, on the sidewalk, for 40 kilometers around the city, the river Spree, the Cathedral, the Cemetery for the Jews that had died, the Central Railway Station of Berlin, which can hold over a million people at a time. Now that makes me wonder where so many travelers could be headed, all at once?

As each building whisked past, I went through a plethora of emotions, from awe to romance, pity, and finally, remorse. Thousands of questions jogging inside my brain—so much trauma this city had been through, and here I was, as if living it's past all over again!

The evening witnessed an open-air performance on the stairway of Pergamon Museum, where my band and I performed to a sea of gyrating audience. A pure feeling of euphoria and contentment. Ah! A day well spent.

Day three was an exotic date with a handsome German counsel friend, Alfred, from a firm I do business with. The gentleman had planned an elaborate cruise down the river Spree in a motor launch, where wine, cheese, and fruits flowed in abundance. We had a heady afternoon with music—live piano orchestrating romantic tunes as if to court a lady!

It made me do some mental gymnastics, although the wine kept fogging the mind, and the breathtaking scenes distracted me constantly. I wondered why women keep investing in dates the way men keep investing in the stock market. My question, as always, came to a dead-end, with no answers!

Day four, was a sumptuous tour of the historical center of the federal capital, on the trail of scenes of World War II, past arches of the city railroad, the old port, through the Museum Island, with seagulls plucking at a catch on the shores of the river, via New Berlin, old national gallery. Further on to Nikolai district, to Bellevue Castle. All spiced up with absorbing anecdotes and events by our able guide! It was a perfect setting to jump up, pick up the mike, and croon the lyrics of Michael Bublé's *Sway*, to the strains of the piano, and did I let the opportunity slip past? No, *sire*!

Having heard of *Breakfast at Tiffany's*, it was weird sitting and devouring breakfast right at the top of legislation! Yes, our final daybreak meal was on top of the German parliament, Reichstag building, and what a meal it was, with a panoramic view of the whole city. Reichstag dome is the iconic large glass dome at the top of the building. The dome has a 360-degree view of the surrounding Berlin cityscape.

The last night was a riotous carnival theme, a funfair which is there all year round at Kulturbrauerei, in the outskirts of Berlin. We had to take the local tube to the venue. Thank holy heavens for chivalrous escorts, or else, what would we, poor damsels dressed in evening gowns, do? It was an adventure, i.e., the tube trip to the venue itself, and the fair was exactly what I had thought it would be, with bumping car rides, spinning the wheel of fortune, where yours truly, struck the cupid thrice, which suddenly rang the theme *"LOVE IS IN THE AIR"* in my ears!

The three hundred square yard area was splattered with cuisines from all across the globe, games, the derby, which I shamelessly lost, balloon popping, posing for the camera, gingerbread cakes as take away, dominos, and gifts galore!

Someone once addressed me as an interesting mix of facts and fantasy, and I guess the child within me enjoyed even the last evening to the hilt! Isn't that what life is all about?

My Berlin trip had come to a climax, but Hamburg was about to begin! I savored every moment of the journey, the history, the memoirs, and the people. It was as though Berlin had offered a delectable palette and I had relished it down to the last morsel!

Reichstag Building, German legislative building

Trabant Cars

Trabant Cars

CHAPTER

04

A Serial Dater, a Man on the Menu - *Next, Please!*

I f only I had the knack of killing time without injuring eternity, I would not have become a Serial Dater!

    A serial dater (SD) and a serial killer (SK) have a peculiar similarity. They both kill or date to increase a number on their list. The SK for the sheer thrill of seeing blood, and a serial dater because she is either bored to death with nothing consequential to do, or is in search of her Mr. Right. After every date, my heart would pound out loud, "Next, please!" Just as a serial killer's does, hunting the next victim. Apologies if the likeness sounds sinister. But that was my exact intention.

The purpose of dating was finding my Mr. Right. My dates always ended in a QPH, i.e., an invented terminology for "Quick Peck and Hug" ☺, and nothing beyond. After 13 dates in a row, with different men, a terrible realization dawned upon me: I was turning into a dating maniac, all roads leading nowhere!

Then again, it would not be totally correct to say *leading nowhere*. This roller coaster ride of dates, that probably began in search of my Mr. Precise, eventually did lead to something significant, and that was an analysis of the types of men coexisting with us in society! They say that women are a queer species... well, let me elucidate on what men are all about!

I have zeroed down on the fact that most men as opposed to women are a very peculiar sex. They have traits that only disengaged singles like me can unravel, layers after layers after layers, like a cabbage!

The first assortment is *"Momma's Pets"*. They fidget while talking, not sure of themselves, looking at the ground, avoiding eye contact, and predictably, the mother calls the thirty-five-plus man at least five times to ensure he is coming home for dinner, while he is dining with his date. I had an urge to snatch the phone and cry, "Lady, are you still changing diapers?" Typically, such a man has been dominated by the only woman in his life, his mother, who, although concedes to his materialistic worldly demands, puts a full stop when it comes to choosing his girl. Aha! That's her forte. Ladies, it's better to let the mother cradle the boy, than you crooning the *Whiskey Lullaby to him!* [I beg your pardon, Brad Paisley. Sorry, being a singer, I have to bring up song titles].

The next category is the *"Married buddy"* ones who come in huge numbers, as singles are scanty. They pretend to be your bosom pals and inevitably pull up the same old traditional sob story of being stuck in a crumbling marriage, with a nagging, malicious wife. I wanted to give him a run down, "Honey, after marriage, all women are bitches." Pardon my language. So, careful, girls; lend a patient ear, not falling prey to the trap being laid to get laid! Oh yes! What a charmer? Sigh! How he makes you wish he was not married. Though he has a way with words, women, and wooing, toughen your heart and sing this song, "There he goes, there he goes again!" [due apologies, Sixpence None the Richer band!]

Falling in sequence is the *"Big Fat Liar"*. He pretends to fall in love at first sight, totally head over heels, claiming to be the most available bachelor in town, almost immediately proposing marriage to you. Probably men have learned over the years, that not the G-spot but the word "marriage" is the fragile spot for most women. Your heart flutters like a little teenage girl in love for the first time [although it's the umpteenth], you almost decide to give in, when one day, suddenly, you call him at the office and discover, to your horror, that he has made a trip to the hospital for his wife's second delivery!

That was the turning point. Now I wanted to turn to serial killing for a change. If somebody had paid a handsome ransom, tempting enough, I would have certainly gone ahead with the assassination game. Alas!

The next variety is the *"Confused One"*. A man who is terrified of committing to a relationship. He has had a bad liaison and that maketh him wary. He adores you and openly declares his affection for you, says I love you ten times a day, but then, he loves his independent status—his so-called freedom, the money he splurges on himself, his damned single life. In a nutshell, he wants to bake his cake and eat it too! No point waiting, lass, he will never say the words that will make your world turn around. So, move on, cherishing your singlehood.

The last array, which I am going to mention here, is the *"Macho Gym Hunk"*. He rules the world with swaggering super confidence, going for the kill each time like a bull, but only where hot girls for flirting and dating are concerned. When it comes to settling down, it has to be simple, homely wife material. No point opting for a man who would undoubtedly try to change you later. Drop him like he's hot! Drop him like he's hot! [again, apologies, Snoop Dogg!]

In case there are some lucky blokes out there who have been out on dates with me and yet have not been featured on this relevant piece of paper, then presume you are the providential ones, I have loved spending my afternoon or evening with! So, don't sweat over it.

Well, the thesis on serial dating and tips to combat situations could go on forever. If serial dating has done nothing, it has at least left me richer with experience and a sixth sense to gauge men and planted the desire within me to turn into a serial killer.

Well, I guess, as they say, most men are alive because it's ILLEGAL TO SHOOT THEM! Gentlemen, no offense there. Peace out!

CHAPTER

05

A Brush with Lesbianism!!!!!

"Help! I am being molested!" the girl ran out screaming, tripping all over herself. By whom? The obvious question. "By this lady out here!" swiftly came the answer!

The victim in question, yours truly, the victimizer, a robust, tri-pack, beefy, masculine, macho... *woman*, four feet some inches in totality! My benign self-towering just a couple of inches above her!

Trust me, not a soul swallowed a word I mumbled, taking it to be a case of madwoman gone absofuckinlutely crazy!

If a woman makes a pass at a woman, what's the victim woman to do? We all have grown up learning the exact manner to react when an Eve is teased by an Adam, but when the Adam in question is a *he-woman,* what kind of reaction should be elicited by the target according to the norms?

I say, handling a man trying to *paw your humble self* [being quite an authority at that now☺] is relatively an easier undertaking than tackling a pure-bred macho woman, possessing an extra Y chromosome, or maybe injected with an overdose of progesterone! It's a mission impossible, and I will tell you why, precisely.

I had accepted to host an event being held at a weird venue in the outskirts of Delhi, just because the package being offered was irresistible. No sooner than I entered the setting, did I start regretting my decision.

It was a clichéd crowd of scruffy men, reeking of beer more than cologne, the deep Haryanvi brawl, heavily desi accented English, the *ijj* and *becojj* thrown randomly, in desperate measures to strike a conversation with me, as I seemed to be the only classy woman around [I take the liberty of proclaiming myself so, with no modesty]. The female quotient was low, and those in attendance were just as disheveled as their male counterparts!

"Today your dignity is at stake, girl," rang a voice in my plodding heart, *"get your defense mechanism ready against these ogres!"*

Little did I envisage, my war was to be raged against a genus of my own species, *a female!* As I tried to do a round of questions on the microphone, suddenly I felt an arm clasp my waistline and hold it in a tight grip, yanking me closer to its face, enveloped in the putrid stench of whiskey!

Immediate reaction: I wrenched myself free and turned around to slap what I thought was a midget of a man. I stopped midway, confused, glaring at the mop of cropped hair, in rugged jeans and shirt, with a young girl by his side. Not wishing to embarrass my organizer, I snapped, *"Sir, will you behave, please?"*

"I am nat a sirrr, I am maddam!" came an unruly answer.

"Come, babby, gi me the mike!" It croaked in my ear, *"I vant to siing a saung far you! Yu aar beauttifool!"*

Not wanting to sound rude, as I was on duty, I politely put the mike next to those wretched lips, but there was no stopping the uncouth hooligan, as the microphone was yanked from my clasp and the audience was subjected to the worst of voices in the history of croaking, in my honor [love songs in Hindi!].

As if the anguish was not enough, the unscrupulous wretch threw the mike, ordered the disc jockey to start spinning, and hauled me all across the floor with my wrist in an iron-like grip, twisting and twirling me to *Tally ho! Tally ho!*

My humble self, spinning like a top, going round and round in circles, a meek lamb [so unlike me], pretending not to be in shock, struggling to break the hand lock, while all the time trying to maintain a composed exterior, as I was a professional emcee here!

Omigosh! What was this? I suddenly see a pair of filthy *black smoke infested lips* planning to attack my cheeks, with people watching, amused? Desperate, I shrieked and shoved and accidentally banged my head against a column [ouch, it still hurts] and ran out screaming, "HELP!!!!" I wouldn't have been surprised if The Beatles themselves had descended that night as my knights in shining armor, such was my plight!

Mission impossible, now you see what I meant? Ironically, I ran into the same he-woman, at a show a few days back. *"Salmate! Thees ijj deshtiny!"* she yelped, and before I could gather my wits, I was seized in a bear-like, unyielding hug! Soulmate? My foot! Dude, our destinies don't collide, as I am perfectly straight. Well, as long as her lips did not plan to lodge onto mine, *I will survive*[with due respect to Gloria Estefan]

I have been an LGBTQ supporter, have spoken in their favor on All India Radio, and got myself banned from the airwaves several times [I accept I am notorious, and our government channel can never predict what I have in store for them☺!]. I have also been a part of the peer group-right movement, for as long as I can recollect, but when it comes to a lip lock, a body rock, with a woman, all I can say is,

For you, I may be hot,
To be cooked in a chicken pot,
And you may like to dance the funky chicken with me,
I'm not your bait, nor your date,
Coz baby I scream 'n shout, don't you see,
I'm STRAIGHT, STRAIGHT, STRAIGHT!

Dear readers - I would certainly appreciate sensible and nonsensical reactions to such a situation. What would you girls do?

Taming a man is easy, but taming of a shrew?

CHAPTER

06

Jane Austen Revisited - A Fairytale Romance

March 8, 2014, at 8:27 AM

A new fiction piece, written by me, as I wanted to bring my imagination to life. It is dedicated to all women and the wonderful men who have such partners, in their lives. I AUTHOR MY GIFT TO YOU... HAPPY WOMEN'S DAY.

It was a sunny autumn afternoon as the cool wind rustled the ravenous red leaves on the lofty trees in Hyde Park, London. Sunday was the day, I always planned lazy long strolls in the park with nothing but leisure on my vacant mind. The breeze ruffled up my crimson flower print cotton dress and caressed my hair gently as though beckoning me into an unforeseen reverie.

The heady fragrance of freshly mowed grass and the sound of chirping birds, painted just the perfect backdrop, on the canvas of a blooming romance, waiting to take contours, with all the colors of ardor. I softly slipped off my moccasins and decided to walk barefoot on the green grass, moist with a little dew from last night.

"Feels succulent, doesn't it??"

I was jerked out of my musing, by a deep baritone male voice, which appeared by my side from almost nowhere. Not being used to any other company in my moments of placidity, *as this was my time with myself*, I was a tad agitated, as I looked up to perceive where the vocals emanated from.

The frame that was walking beside me, the midget, was a towering six feet something, fair, athletically built, enticingly handsome countenance with a cherubic smile, which instantly set my apprehensions at ease.

"Yes, divinely so," I smiled back.

"So, you come here often?" he quizzed.

"Sundays."

"You reside nearby?" he asked.

"Yes, just around the corner, three blocks from here."

"I go by the name Wales, Devon Wales."

"Wendy, Gwendolyn Harper."

"Hmmm... very musical," he quipped.

"I beg your pardon?" I was startled by his nonchalant reaction.

"Your name!" he reiterated.

"What else would you expect from a singer?" promptly came my reply.

"Oh, now that's what I call providence. You are a singer and I a connoisseur of music, although I must admit I cannot belt out, even the do-re-mi in perfect melody!"

Unable to comprehend the ease with which his banter flowed, I burst into a lilting laugh.

Oh my God, was this my feminine side that I had almost suppressed over the years being evoked, suddenly, with this stranger?

It was as easy as that. This man possessed the sporadic knack of leading any chat into the comfort zone. Although it has never been my tendency to have dialogs with aliens, it seemed most natural at that moment.

We have been warned as little girls not to talk to strangers, particularly good-looking ones, as the unknown sweet talkers are the lady's worst enemy. They entrap, ensnare, misuse, and walk on, having experienced that all my life. Yet, somehow, this time it seemed very different.

Our conversation lasted for three hours or more and not one moment went by, where there was a feeling of boredom or to escape his company, which was nothing but alluring. He spun anecdotes and engrossing yarns from his past. In those placid hours, I learned he was divorced, single as of now, with no attachments, and he owned a shipping company with offices all across the globe. His main office was just next to Times Square London.

Somewhere in the midst of all this, a question galloped through my whimsical mind. What was such a man, with the assets he owned, including irresistible looks, alluring sense of humor, doing in the company of a Bohemian such as myself? But I was quick enough to brush this query of my quirky mind aside with equal deftness with which it had crept in!

Reminiscing the moments spent with him and with all questions doing mental gymnastics in my brain, I ambled a dazed walk to my little one-room apartment as twilight eclipsed the sky. The hopeless romantic that I am, I decided to go with the flow and see what fate had in store for me.

From then on, Sundays became a ceremonious day to look forward to, when I would meet this amiable stranger, talk on relentlessly for hours, share laughter, weekly headlines, stories of my musical gigs, my sketches of new cities I traveled, his tales of his latest business ventures, meetings with new people, cultures, places he visited.

At times, he would seek my counsel on important matters, which I found a bit unexpected, but felt honored nonetheless; I became an important part of his life slowly. He never talked much about his family, and I was careful not to tread on marshy land.

We had exchanged numbers, and often I would receive hilarious texts from him and a call once in a while. I so started looking forward to those messages and phone calls, which would send my heart into a frenzy! Even a smiley from him would render butterflies in my stomach!

What was this? Was I falling in love with a man I barely knew for two months? "He is so funny," my heart replied. "But what if he has skeletons in his closet?" quipped my brain. 'What if..."

"Shhh, live for the moment, girl" was an echo in the remote realms of my brain, that my heart was sending—and *live*, I did.

Finally, after four months, which seemed the longest wait in my life—but then, that was his most alluring quality, as he never rushed into things—he asked me out on a date, a perfect evening on the banks of River Thames. He whisked me off on his private yacht, a captivating candlelit dinner on the decks, as wine flowed and live musicians, he especially hired for the evening, played my favorite melodies, a picture-perfect ensemble for an unforgettable night, emblazoned in my memory. As a grand finale, he had mistletoe hanging surreptitiously in the cabin below. Just as an unassuming me, entered to wash my hands, he scooped me up and devoured my mouth in a gentle deep kiss—our first kiss! A kiss like none I had ever experienced before! And it made everything official.

No evening has ever been more flawless in my entire life, which was a myriad of broken disastrous relations; men have been abusive, users, callous, and foolhardy, with no respect for the woman. Most men who seem *appealing at first turn out to be utterly appalling.* Or else they have been so relentlessly entombed in the burdens of their past, it has left them burned out completely with nothing to offer, to the new relationship. So, for me, it was a fairytale, I always dreamed of. And I savored it!

Dev made me realize that for any kind of lasting relationship, you have to have a lot of passions in common. And we had one too many. Undoubtedly, the age-old theory that *opposites attract*, does not hold well in the modern biosphere. For, travel was our appetizer, music was the staple diet, writing and reading were the entree, painting and doing house interiors were the mutual love we cherished, good exotic cuisine our lust, photography the hobby, cooking for each other, a pleasant time pass, and we both shared an inert hunger for good clothes and fashion. I could simply go on elucidating. Each day was a new discovery about the other.

As grownups, we often blackmail our hearts into doing things our brains won't allow, which includes following a diet. My brain says no, no, no, but my heart says go, go, go. Devon never stopped me from doing or eating anything I liked. The best part: he hated diets and loved every curve in my body, even the parts I found unflattering and fat. It brought to mind Billy Joel's *I love you just the way you are*. This endeared him more to me.

When I queried "why me?", he merely replied, "Every little thing you do is magic." "You are *effortlessly comical* [I took offense to that at first, but understood what he meant], adorable, intelligent, gifted, amorous, affectionate, reasonable, humanitarian, you are gorgeous, yet above all, you are not even aware of how pretty you are. All compliments you dismiss with a blush, and that is so captivating! In a nutshell, *my complete child woman!*" He loved my silly absentminded whacky antics, and never got exasperated or upset.

He couldn't stop laughing, at my antics, the evening after dinner in a fancy restaurant, he went to get his big black car out of the parking, as he did not believe in valets. I am a total ignorant imbecile when it comes to recognizing car brands except for my favorite, Vintage Jaguar. A big black car stopped in front of me. The absentminded me, simply opened the door, jumped in, and said, "Let's go, let's go, honey!" An astonished gentleman in the car looked on, in total perplexity! Devon, in his car behind us, was in splits, as he understood exactly what happened!

I asked him to come to my concert at Piccadilly Square. He did. Somehow, I felt like a proud peahen exhibiting my guy to my band members and other friends. I could sense the envy and simultaneous insecurity in their aura. Wendy, the poor loner who spent almost all her time, her holidays alone, now had this extravagant gentleman, who was a bundle of fun with no paucity of manners and, to top it all, well off too…

Again, I amused him with my inadvertent antics. While singing on the stage, so lost in my performance, I never realized I had reached the edge of the stage, as the heavy-duty lights utterly blinded me. I fell off the four feet high stage, straight into the confetti blasts! As I struggled to get out my heels stuck in the confetti cylinder, he rushed to help me up, but I brushed it off and shrugged as though nothing happened and carried on singing, with élan and panache. He stood there, thoroughly entertained, holding my hand and beaming!

He loved every part of my concert, my music, my singing, my performance, and also my big plummet! He hugged me in an affectionate cuddle as I stepped off the stage and whispered, "With you around, there is never a dull moment." *It was then I realized we were two of a kind.* Lord! It was all too perfect to be true. There had to be a catch somewhere.

Shoo, shoo away, you *wicked logical left side of the brain*! My fairytale *will* have a happy ending.

And it did. 21st of February, on my birthday, nine months from the day we met at Hyde Park, at 7 am, I hear a choir singing the *Wedding March* below my house. Confused, I tumble out of bed and peep out the window to witness an open-top Jaguar 1948 model, trust me, in pristine white, with wedding marchers behind. A dashing Devon, looking dapper in white, with white lilies in his hand, was screaming on the streets below, "Wendy, I love you to bits, will you let me chaperon you the rest of my miserable life?" A scene right out of *Pretty woman!*

Tears of joy, a bit of skepticism, poured relentlessly in a downpour over my bedraggled face as I scrambled down the stairs, in my pajamas, straight into his welcoming arms, as he seized me in a warm embrace, with a muffled "yes" escaping my lips!

We got married the same week on the beaches of Hawaii with just a pastor, him, and me. It's been 15 years today, and each day is a new fairytale to be breathed, believed, and experienced, with us more in love with the other, each rising sun of our lives.

You can write your happy endings, provided you *believe* in them, when you pen them down, or should I say type them down. The whole universe will then collaborate and conspire to bring what you want to you.

They say, *your* life *can* be a fairytale, only if you write your own story just the way you want it—*perfect*—the way I wrote mine!

[At certain places, I was tempted to give a wicked twist to the story with the line "what lurked in the dark cervices of Devon's life, little did Wendy know…" but I decided no thriller; keep it a plain, simple rom-com!!Lol]

Credit for the line "Everything she does is magic" goes to Rajnish Pathak -the hilarious

hijacker! Thank you!

CHAPTER

07

"HUSSY"... TOE... PHASI!!!! [If She laughs she is trapped]

January 29, 2010, at 1:23 AM

As you unconsciously glide that smooth coffee-flavored lip gloss on that perfect pout, your mind just wanders beyond the reflection in the mirror, conjuring up thoughts and haphazardly placing the pieces of the jigsaw called "a single woman's life"!

What would be the exact preconceived notions about you, of the man, who has offered to take you out for dinner? As per my deduction, based on a series of disastrous dull dates, acquaintances, and evenings out, I have positively come to a conclusion: when a man spots a gorgeous, steaming hot, sensuous, single [or maybe not so single], bold, outgoing woman, who dresses as she likes and speaks her mind out, especially in the glamor industry, he invariably jumps to a conclusion, pinning the term "available hussy" on her!

I do beg your pardon for using such an odious word. Indeed, I should be the one most offended, as it demeans the very essence of the whole of womanhood, considering the fact I represent the gender and hold the placard of belonging to the species high up, so very strongly!

But such unpleasant instances, have been my past experience. My personal data states that 88% of the men look down upon the entire species of women of this variety. When they discover that women like me are quite the contrary to their fancy, their obsessive curiosity in the gentle species, takes a two-way course, either it gets further ignited, trying to obtain the impossible, or ends up shunning them and maligning the lady's public image, at times even insinuating her in public. [trust me, most of the men are bigger bitches than us, ignoring the fact that they are gay or straight! That's immaterial.], trying to protect their own macho illustration in the community.

Such was this night's experience with this gentleman from the entertainment industry, with whom I had been casually interacting on the telephone for the last few months. Incidentally, he had landed in my home away from home, Mumbai, got himself invited to my place to pick me up and take me out for dinner, thinking he would get lucky! I wonder how callously I had shredded his optimism to pieces, as I could conclude from his text later in the night, where after being turned down by me, he inquired, whether he could hope for some *adult fun* in a certain very well-known party joint, in Mumbai. My answer?? "Well, depends upon the levels of your desperation and the woman's morals!" 😊

All through the evening, he kept dropping hints and names of infamous women in the glamor world, and their not so illustrious acts and filthy escapades, all the while trying to size me up, until, finally, I had to make my point, of where and what I stood for, crystal clear, though not without a little effort, retaining my dignity and salvaging whatever pride was left in my genus.

Well, maybe there are women in our line of work, who hunger for instant wealth, instant success, instant fame [like Instant Maggi 2-minute noodles], and the perks that come along with it, go for instant gratification and accept the title [of a hussy] with grace, succumbing and eventually, in the process, bringing the name of our genus down. They probably don't envisage that what one accomplishes through pedantic effort [not that their approach is effortless😊!], aptitude, hard work, fortitude, and perseverance goes a long way to stay with you, your entire life. But does that typify that all ladies are the same?

So, ladies, buckle up [in the right places]! It's up to us to take a stand. We are game to blame the situations and circumstances. However, there is no such thing as a "circumstance." It's all about tackling a situation and how tactfully you deal with it. Try to bear in mind: every day is a new day and a new opportunity!

I repeat as I have said umpteen times before: *"learn to love yourself, it's the beginning of a lifelong romance!"* So, make it a habit to look at yourself in the mirror every day and chime, "I love you, baby. I will do nothing to tarnish your self-esteem. I promise to cherish and pamper you like a baby, because you are too precious!"

So, in a nutshell, round up your lips, not for nips, but to let out the monosyllable with only two letters of the alphabet in it… "NO," and the world will lie at your feet, if not beyond [wink]!!!!

Hont ghuma, citi bajaa, citii bajaake bol "O bhaiya no no no!!"

CHAPTER

08

Miss Misfortune - Part 2

Dated 28th March 2009

Didn't I always confess I am Miss Misfortune? One more amusingly unfortunate incident to prove it...

The movie *Confessions of a Shopaholic* must have been conceptualized, with yours truly, in mind... On a breezy and overcast Saturday evening, I had been shopping for over an hour, at the ever infamous Sarojini Nagar market for nightwear, because this is one place where you get inexpensive, rugged body-friendly fabrics, sculpted into comfortable ensembles, at rock bottom prices. Being a single woman, with no man to glare at me and my humble self, while I sleep, I prefer unflattering, cheap yet stress-free prêt nightwear, how much ever, I might flaunt my figure in expensive designer stuff while strutting in parties!

While winding the shopping up, I spot some delicious fresh fruit, waiting to go inside my basket.

Suddenly, I feel a drop go plop on my head. It's about to rain. No way! I was not going to let a light drizzle, play wet blanket with my plans to go full swing on a fruit diet. So, despite the skies crying out a desolate warning, I make a desperate attempt to purchase some really sumptuous fresh fruit, only to be almost caught in a downpour…

But then, I am "Vandy"!

Nothing can get the better of me, not time, destiny, or even nature! That's why, before the Gods above, burst the tankers, I was safely inside my tiny buggy, snug with my purchases, and lit the ignition and reversed the vehicle, which was parked on top of a sidewalk near the apartments.

Alas! As Mum had always said, "Are you happy, honey?? Don't worry, you will soon get over it!" Blinded by the sudden cloudburst, the left-hand-side tyre, flies off the twelve-inch high concrete, and is left spinning in the air, with the rod connecting the set of two front tyres, landing, with a devilish conspiracy that the duo [the tyres, I mean] had hatched against me, on the pavement. The car was left balancing, to save its precious life!

Now what? Visibility is next to zero, it's late in the night, with hardly a soul around. After debating, and relentlessly trying my level best to reverse or move the car forward, the only outcome was that the stubborn wheel, spun, churned, whipped up some fresh creamy wet mud, and gyrated disobediently in the air, as if to mock me and sing in chorus, "You took us for a ride, girl, now we spin you around!" with the car not budging a centimeter.

Then, just out of nowhere, a man in a Wagon R notices, slows down, observes, and… just passes by, wiping off the optimistic smile on my countenance.

But no, he stops just behind me, parks, walks up in the deluge, and volunteers to help the lady in distress.

Now it was my turn to scoff at the wheels! Ha! You two nincompoops! The gods are watching me. See? He launched his messenger [yahooooooo-ooo.co!] to take care of me!

In no time, the quick-witted man had formulated an arrangement, propped up the wicked wheel on bricks, created a slant, reversed my car, handed me my keys, tipped his hat, oops! Sorry, no, there was no hat there! I do get carried away into the Victorian era at times such as these!

With me thanking him profusely for turning into my knight in shining armor, we exchanged smiles and were on our way!

Where?? To our individual destinations, of course!

With me, drenched to the bone, yet happily spinning through the torrent, humming, "Raindrops keep falling on my head! And nothing can get me down!!"

So, in a nutshell, I am MISS MISFORTUNE AND FORTUNE ALWAYS GIVES ME A MISS. BUT THEN WHEN I MISS FORTUNE, FORTUNE STARTS MISSING ME! ARE YOU MISSING SOMETHING? NO SWEAT, LET'S TAKE IT FROM THE TOP!!

CHAPTER

09

Slavery, Thy Name is Woman? is Your Guy a "BI"? – Reflect, Woman

August 7, 2012, at 1:56 AM

Slavery, thy name is woman, when she falls headlong in love! Now, to how many women does this apply? Raise your hands, or forever hold your silence? Is it really true that women when *blinded by the bourka of love* over their eyes become mere puppets in the hands of the man?

Is it the intrinsic nature of man to pursue a woman that catches his fancy, wine, dine, and win her over with his pledge of undying love, wooing her with a phony claim of "understanding her emotions," showing her stars and *their future together*, planning *their offspring*, their home, a blessed family in unison, all of which is a woman's innermost dream, and eventually walking all over her, draining her psychologically, physically, spiritually, mentally, financially, leading her to break her ties with her loved ones? And in due course dumping and walking out of her life, without so much as an explanation, justification, or rationalization?

The woman is left 99 out of 100 times wondering what went wrong. Flabbergast, trying to cope with the demoralized feeling that she is incapable, incomplete, a sure shot loser?

Now, how many times, is a woman to be subjected to such traumatic, harrowing encounters till she finally breaks down.

The male species is blessed with the propensity of switching off their emotions, as and when they feel like, as per their convenience, and switching on all over again, when they start missing the woman, in the future, or when they have that orgasmic adrenaline rush, seeing their ex in a new diva avatar!

Most wounded girls end up building a graveyard of their, *good love gone bad*, with a bunch of sympathetic *female or gay friends*, over packets of chips and empty wine bottles, expecting the pain to get buried amongst these graves, unfortunately, ending up in gaining oodles of Kilograms and a disfigured shape!

But a few emotionally brawny types, *the tough cookies like me, tumble*, levitate again, dust the rags of their dignity, take a deep breath, and stride on, once more! Ahoy, girl, way to go!

But what does go wrong in such perfectly seeming relationships? Does the man get bored of seeing the committed side of the girl, whom he thought was fun, or is it just the thought of the woman getting serious, unnerving him that he scuttles like a terrified bunny? So many unanswered questions left to be answered by yourself.

For the girl, her life starts revolving around her man. "Oh my God, that's his favorite brand of cigarettes," or "his favorite juice brand." "Omigosh! He doesn't have any casuals to wear," "his perfume has exhausted," "chicken lollipop, honey? I can definitely learn that for you!" Somewhere down the line, her identity is lost. Now she is living her life his way, and only for him, to make him happy. She becomes female version of MR SO AND SO, rather than being a Miss. Herself! Hence *"Miss"ing* the whole point of being a woman with individuality!! She is the giver and he the taker. A selfish man, not tuned in to her needs, and what does he have to offer in return? Complaints and his woes, and miseries dumped on to the already overburdened girl's shoulders!

Men may beg to differ, stating there are tigresses out there in the jungle, who are the *exact prototype* of the men described above, but I still believe the count of ruthless men, outnumbers the women on a scale of one to ten!

Maybe the men who suffer at the hands of a woman are *sanctified with that extra sensitive female X chromosome* that acquaints them with their feminine attribute [LOL]. God! When will women like me find this extra X chromosome man, *without him turning out to be completely gay*!:)

Now, here again, that GAY word is something to be wary of... no prejudice here *as my best friend*s are *true gays*, but men who swing both ways and want their male image to be fortified in society choose girls [I am aware of many victims amongst my acquaintances] to protect their "masculine" illustration by sincerely entering a *fake wedlock of marriage*, yet *go for a tight gay arse* whenever they have an opportunity to do so, as that is where their preferences lie. The lady might be celebrating the fact, that she managed to catch a single, available, loving, caring *man who does not look at other women,* while the truth may be quite the contrary! Hahahaha!

Ladies, you never know when a bisexual, in the guise of a straight man may be wooing you, to perfection! What are such men to be called? Gay, straight, or bisexual? Important issue: how do we women assess them in the crowd? This is a question that has been driving me nuts!

You want a man with his feminine sensitivities alive and yet are perturbed by the fact he may turn out to be gay! What a catch 22 situation!

What we need is a man who is macho enough to protect his beloved with all sincerity and feminine enough to serve her tea in bed. Without turning us, into their humble servants! That's it! This is the undemanding desire of a simple-hearted girl like me. Now is that too much to ask for?

Finally, all and sundry applaud me for being a brilliant writer. Well, is going through a natural process, of traumatic life experiences necessary, to make a chiseled writer out of you? Then, in a good way, I have all these painful, bitter, sweet, hilarious encounters, to whom I owe the credit for all the pieces that have gone down on paper. Halleluiah! Keep them coming, Krishna, and let's celebrate each moment of life—*sweet, salted, bitter, crisp, soggy, or tasteless— as it falls on our platter and tingles the palate.*

But someone please give me the mantra of falling in love without getting the emotions too entangled as to become the trailing shadow of the man you love! Amen.

CHAPTER

10

Mystic Magical Fairyland: Glastonbury

February 7, 2011, at 4:50 PM
Mystic GLASTONBURY

Being a soul craving for adventure, spirituality, friends, and exploring the unknown, mysticism of the world, my heart leaped up when I received a call from my clairvoyant and angel therapist, Sunita Singad Rustam, saying, "Vandy, I am taking a pilgrimage to Glastonbury. Seven girls are going, I am falling short of one. Would you be interested??"

Pilgrimage in Glastonbury? I always thought it was a Mecca of music festivals. I replied, "Who all are going?" I learned two of my very close college buddies, Aarti and Divya, were accompanying too. That closed it; it was reason enough to immediately send my reply, in the affirmative! This holiday meant spending quality time, away from the so-called stiff upper lip society of main London, away from the Gucci's, Bottega Veneta's, Louis Vuitton's, and five stars of the world. A welcome break in the virgin countryside, with a circle of good friends.

Mind you, if you, like me, are one of those depleting few, who ebb and flow between the snooty, hoity-toity, upper-class social circuit and can just as easily slip into the guise of a backpacker, *this is the perfect getaway for you!*

Mark my words, if you like magic, Glastonbury is the sabbatical destination for you. It is a *"mystic, myth, and legend backdrop"* that weaves its way through everything you will visit and see at Glastonbury.

How to get there:

The bunch of us eight girls plus our guide Suni and her husband, Rustam Joseph, embarked on the Jet Airways flight from Mumbai to Heathrow, London Central. From then onwards, there was a coach hired to take us to Glastonbury. For those who enjoy escapades, you could try the bus or the train, but then please travel light! Stow away those expensive Dior shoes and sheepskin Armani jackets!

A rugged pair of jeans, a couple of tees, trainers, a warm jacket, and maybe a dress for a romantic unexpected evening that just might crop up, with flirty sandals, is just enough to weave magic into your sojourn.

The quickest but most expensive option, is by train from London's Paddington Station to Castle Cary, approximately 1½ hour. The cheapest option between London and Glastonbury, is the National Express coach that takes around 4 hours to do the journey direct.

If you wish to make the most of this holiday, plan your itinerary for 5 to 6 days.

So, unlike my luxurious high-flying holidays, we checked into *Pilgrims Bed & Breakfast*, which had quaintly comfy rooms. A lovely couple, Clair and Brian Carlton, run the place. It was awesome to hear them spin tales and anecdotes of angels and mysticism at breakfast each morning, that Claire meticulously prepared for us. What could be better than having the comfort of home to live in, while abroad?

About Glastonbury & places to visit:

It's a compact town where everything worth seeing is within walking distance and it can easily occupy a full day of anybody's time, or much more if you are one of the lividly quixotic photographers, clubbed with journal keepers, like me. *I simply love romancing a town irately,* enthusiastically living its legends, breathing its history, and letting my soul absorb its culture! That way, one can fantasize about being dressed up in pagan costumes of eighteenth-century England, *trudging the streets in pinafores and frilly bishop sleeved white shirts!*

One of the refreshing aspects of Glastonbury is, that it is not over-commercialized and very few large coaches visit.

High Street has enough pubs and places to eat to satisfy most people's palates.

Most memorable though, will be the "new age" mystic shops and the hippy-like characters, that have made Glastonbury their home.

High Street is strewn with shops that sell semi-precious to precious stones, exotic costumes, robes, monk capes, you may even spot a random *store selling magic potions* with a wizard, brewing a stew in an iron cauldron! I so desperately wanted to pick the bottle labeled *"love potion no 9"!* Alas, my overprotective friends knew, to what extent I could go when it came to experimenting, and I was deprived of picking a vial! There are also a lot of angel product stores selling fairies and angel figurines and angel dust and magic crystals, *everything straight out of a fairytale book.*

Wearyall Hill & the thorn tree:

Wearyall Hill is a long narrow ridge, to the southwest of Glastonbury. On the hill is the Holy Thorn. The original was said to have blossomed from the staff of Joseph of Arimathea, who legend says, visited Glastonbury, carrying the Holy Grail. He arrived, weary (hence Wearyall Hill), planted his staff in the ground, and it immediately blossomed.

The tree is seen as sacred, blossoming at Christmas and Easter, marking the birth and resurrection of Jesus Christ.

Oh, how my whimsical heart believed and drank in, every piece of information, that was being doled out generously to me, as *I envisioned my silhouette standing next to Joseph of Arimathea on the Wearyall Hill as one of Jesus' disciples.*

Glastonbury Abbey

Glastonbury Abbey was established as a Benedictine monastery during the years 670 to 678 AD. Before that time, it had existed, for many years, as a Celtic religious center.

According to legend, 2000 years ago, Joseph of Arimathea (Christ's uncle) is supposed to have brought the young Jesus here.

On Joseph's second visit, after Christ's death, he built the *first Christian church,* at Glastonbury Abbey.

Visiting Glastonbury Abbey

Glastonbury Abbey itself is very accessible, positioned just off the main High Street. Looking from the perspective of High Street, you cannot really make out that there is a sprawling 38 acres of property inside.

One can enjoy a royal guided tour of the abbey with a handsome pilot, *draped in Arthurian costume,* that whisks you to the era of King Arthur and the Knights of the Round Table and their quest for the Holy Grail.

As I wandered deeper into the abbey and delved into its history, I could envisage King Arthur and Guinevere riding through the abbey lawns! There was enough material for me to shoot with my camera, as I was all ears, hands, feet, and concentration, trying not to miss any part of the guided tour!

Glastonbury Tor

Tor is the Celtic name for a cone-shaped hill. So, Glastonbury Tor *is a hill* in Glastonbury. The hill is one of the icons of Glastonbury and can be seen from afar. It has become a sacred site for many who believe in it.

It was a weary climb at 5 am to the top of the Tor. But once we reached the zenith, it was the most spectacular sight and elevating sensation. En route, we *encountered two wizards, draped in the pagan monk's robe,* with a staff and an Arthurian sword in their hands, winding their way back, after performing sacred spells and rituals at 4 am, at the Tor! *Why the Tor? Read on to learn the eerie mystery!*

- *The tower* on the Tor is the remnants of a fourteenth-century chapel dedicated to Saint Michael, a replacement for an earlier church destroyed by an earthquake in 1275.
- The chapel is in itself evidence *of the site's pre-Christian roots.*

It was a common practice to build churches on pagan worship sites. Such churches were often dedicated to Michael in his role as spiritual guardian and protector of the people, also called *Arc Angel Michael, who battled Satan [Lucifer] from heaven,* as per the holy Bible

- Dowsing methods have now traced many *ley i.e. power, dragon lines* in the earth that for centuries were known to folklore. These are natural geomagnetic lines in the earth.
- One such ley line called "The Michael line" is so named because most of the churches on it are dedicated to St. Michael, protector of the faith.

The Michael line flows down from the Tor and then passes through the other major Glastonbury sites—Chalice Well, the Abbey, and Wearyall Hill—now isn't that spooky, eh?

The Tor is also supposed to be the place under which the Holy Grail is buried, linked to the Chalice Well.

In ancient times, the Somerset Levels were a shallow, marshy sea. Then, *Glastonbury Tor was an island.*

Legend has it that the Tor is the Island of Avalon, the burial site of King Arthur!

- Viewed close up, its slopes are subtly terraced, and some scholars speculate that it forms a vestige of a *Neolithic labyrinth.*

The Celts called it the Isle of Glass, hence the name *Glas*tonbury, *and believed it was a gateway to the underworld.*

- Yet there are others, like me, who believe a fairyland exists under Tor Hill! So explicitly evident from the size of huge *two feet tall hares* [rabbits] we saw jumping amongst the humongous trees, a scene straight out of Alice and the Mad Hatter's party!

- All said and done for the legends, the energies at the Tor were overpowering.

After some meditation to my dear buddy and guide Michael, and picturesque photography and being frozen to the bone, in the minus degree chill, we headed back to the town, happy, light-hearted, and content. As we commenced the descent, we *noticed massive wing-shaped clouds* waving to us like huge flapping angel feathers. A testimony to the fact our invocations were accepted.

The Chalice Well

According to legend, the Chalice Well is believed to have sprung from the ground at the location where the chalice (the Holy Grail), which Jesus drank from, at the Last Supper and in which drops of his blood were caught, during the Crucifixion, was placed.

The well itself is thought to have been built by the Druids and the water that gushes from it, reddish in color and tasting of iron, has been claimed to have magical healing powers.

The color of the water and the taste, according to legend, is said to symbolize the *iron nails that were used at the Crucifixion.*

The wrought iron emblem on the Chalice Well trap door, with two circles overlapping each other, is a symbol of a passage to the other world.

A high priestess from Glastonbury Goddess Temple, namely Coco, conducted purification, on the bunch of eight overexcited girls, with the magical water. She blessed us, and we all sang hymns singing praises of Mother Earth and her bounty. *This is how enchanting life was 2000 years ago, my mind drifted off into a reverie, reliving each moment of the era gone by.*

The Chalice Well is flanked by sublime gardens, echoing peace, solitude, strewn with benches and little coves where one can just sit, meditate, and reflect. Or, for the dreamier lot, read a book of

Harry Potter and the Goblet of Fire, or ponder like King Arthur as to the whereabouts of the Holy Grail!

The White Spring

Less than 100 meters from the Chalice Well, famous for its red water, flows a second and uniquely related well, the White Spring.

The White Spring is a calcium- and energy-rich well that flows up to the foot of Glastonbury Tor.

The Stonehenge

Our final destination was one of the Seven Wonders of the World, in Amesbury, the Stonehenge. At a glance, it may appear to you as just a pile of stones in a barren field in the middle of nowhere and nothing special.

The Neolithic people-built Stonehenge about *4.5 thousand years ago.*

Stonehenge was not built overnight. This was a project that was built over centuries.

These stones are of various shapes and sizes, from 3 feet to over 9 feet tall, strategically balanced, for thousands of years. Arranged in a specific alignment, to track the lunar cycle.

As in Glastonbury, a number of ley lines crisscross in the center of Stonehenge.

The real purpose of Stonehenge is still not clear.

It was certainly a sacred area, for memorial services to be performed. All the stones at Stonehenge are precisely sited and correlate to significant events of the planet's orbit, like solstices. Religious ceremonies were conducted there as per the solar and lunar cycles.

It was also a place of pilgrimage where people arrived from remote lands.

In the center of the Stonehenge, High Priestess Coco performed a spiritual ceremony and meditation for our wellbeing and prosperity.

➢ The most memorable part was when the gracious priestess, carrying the guitar of a musician whose ashes were scattered over Stonehenge, *asked me to play in the middle of the sacred ritual ground*, as though beckoning the universe to speed up, my magical spiritual and musical journey! *Thank you, Coco, for helping me relive my past and my future at the divine Stonehenge.*

What else to do in Glastonbury

The town is full of fascinating and exciting activities to do. You could check out the list of happenings in the brochures available at the bed and breakfast and enroll in various intriguing workshops and colloquium. They range from a vast variety of music classes to shamanic clubs, to angelology seminars. Knowledge is in abundance; only the will to learn, absorb, and believe is needed. One could enjoy the spree even more if you are a music aficionado and club it with the Glastonbury Music Festival. But if you are a party *clubbing buff*, this is certainly not the town for you.

With that, we came to the culmination of the breathtakingly old-fashioned expedition.

I am sure after reading excerpts from my journal, many struck by wanderlust and haunted, with the lust for exploring the mysteries of the world, would be compelled to take up this numinous holiday.

There is always a little Wicca and a wizard in each one of us, tucked under the covers of social norms and logic. Tell the logical part of your brain to shut up and take a chill pill!

Go ahead and indulge in the realm of angelic mysticism, as it's never too late to awaken the Shamanic Wicca in you! Love and light!

[Thank you, Sunita and Rustam and Aarti dahling!:)]

Vanndana Vaadera at the Abbey

Vanndana Vaadera at the Abbey

Glastonbury Tor

Glastonbury Tor

Coco and Vanndana Vaadera at the Chalice Well Gardens

Sunita, Aarti Bajaj, Smita, Vanndana Vaadera, Rustam, Coco at Stone Henge

CHAPTER

11

The Cat's Tryst With The *Cat*

When I spotted a leopard in front of my car, just a leap AWAY! And a Kodak moment missed.

THE CAT SPOTS THE CAT!

The swishing of a long, glistening, *golden tail*, 40 meters ahead on the road, in the adjacent bushes, which overlooked the valley, made my heart leap with anticipation. The driveway, as one enters the Royal Palms, Aarey Colony, from Powai side, adjoining the deserted, opulent Royal Imperial Hotel, is an isolated one for sure.

This spot is approximately, a startling two kilometers away from my abode. It has been popular for numerous leopard sightings. The proximity to the Borivali National Park, renders this area more prone to catching a glimpse of *tendua*, as sadly, we humans have encroached their terrain.

Ever since I had purchased the tiny nook of mine, in this settlement, I had prayed that I set my eyes on the glorious creature, at least once during my lifetime, up close and personal. The *moment* had arrived. I was excited, thrilled, and tripping with curiosity. Seeing in the zoo is a different scenario, but when out of the blue, next to your living quarters, precipitously, so close, all alone, wild and uninhibited in the pitch dark of the night, not only the proximity but even the concept of witnessing one, was intoxicating.

The adventure freak within me, made me slow my car and turn down the beam. I lightly pressed the accelerator, very slowly purring my engine, gently to move ahead in first gear. As I edged closer, the Leopard jumped on, to the middle of the road, and *swish*! I turned on the headlights in full beam. It gazed at the car, and I felt it was *gawking* into my eyes, as I stared back, mesmerized by its sheer beauty, grandeur, and *lofty* poise!

It was a pure golden shade, rather tawny, with alarmingly, amazing patterned, black rosettes on its lustrous coat. It had yellowish-gray beamers that flashed piercingly toward me.

Our cat eyes met for four beautiful seconds, then instantly I apprehended, I should take a picture of this perfect moment. I guess my reflexes at such nostalgic moments are very sluggish.

I reached out for my mobile. Alas, too late! It was a brand new phone I was trying to get a hang of, and by the time the camera came on, the handsome creature leaped on to the gap in the fragmented ledge, like the Lord of the Kings and disappeared into the pitch dark, abandoned, haunting hotel, leaving me bereft of breath. This was blasphemy indeed. I had missed a Kodak moment!

Although I never reflected on it at that moment, as I thought about it later, I was certainly glad I was inside my car. What would have my reaction been if I had been treading on foot, as I do go for long walks on this side of undulated Royal Palms? I couldn't imagine, for the world of me.

Well, I had been deprived of the privilege of capturing the beast on my camera, but incarcerating it in my memories, was more than enough for me, the nature lusting and wildlife lover. Just the thought of having seen the majestic animal so intimately, in the tamed, or should I rephrase, in the "wild" human inhabitation, left me with a satisfied smile playing on my lips. Now I had a story to narrate in the years to come.

SO, THIS WAS *THE* CAT'S TRYST WITH THE *CAT*! A member of their own feline species.

CHAPTER

12

Arjun On My Mind, Arjun In My Heart!

This last story is a piece of fiction, just to get your imagination running!

The Social networking media has become a kind of weird tool, to bring lonely souls together. But most of the time, it's a medium for horny women stalkers, or even men hunters chancing upon pretty profiles for prey! At record instances, when your luck is at its worst, you will chance upon sleazebags, weighing you down with suggestive disgusting proposals in the inbox.

But if your lady luck is on your side, even one percent, you will accidentally bump into the soul mate, you had been hunting for lifetimes!

It was a sultry monsoon, Wednesday evening in Bombay. After my plethora of meetings, of a strenuous day, I was relaxing with a mug of hot chocolate and browsing through my inbox on Facebook, when I chanced upon a seemingly fascinating message from a handsome countenance, that beamed upon me, through beady black eyes. I was quite used to receiving messages from aliens, with loads of cranky stale opening lines and pick up slogans. I would delete and block them without further contemplation. But somehow, that face, rather than the phrases it rattled off, was something that kept me from deleting the message.

Arjun Singh, okay, a Rajput lad… let's see what proposal he has for me, I smiled. "You are breathtakingly gorgeous, would be the sleaziest introduction line, if I said that, but then I have no words to describe what you are. I have been following your public posts for last 1 year, and finally mustered the confidence to write this message to you. You can't envisage how many drafts of this note I made and tore up. Then finally decided, that I let my libretti flow naturally." This line brought a sincere smile to my lips. I was used to the blah blah blahs. But the "torn drafts" part of the message, really tugged warmly, at my heart's chord.

It continued, "Under normal circumstances I am normal, but today, I am abnormally abnormal, as this is the brashest thing, I have done to send an epilogue, to a perfectly unfamiliar lady, and this is usually not me, the *egoistic* Arjun. But a year of following your profile, has somehow transformed me, humbled me, to see a woman in a very different light.

Strangely Vandy, if I may address you that, you may not be aware, but your posts, your photos, your wit, humor, intelligence reflecting in your original status updates, coupled with your sensuality, plugged in with inexplicable innocence, all being very opposite, alluring qualities, has touched and changed the lives of many I am sure, I being the best paradigm. So finally, the pertinent question, can I be added in your honored friend list?"

There, that was it. Without so much as a thought, I hit the accept button.

He was funny, charming, anything but boring. The alacrity with which the conversation flowed could even turn a corpse in its grave. We soon became chat buddies on the Blackberry messenger. Oh, technology, how benevolent art thou, that thou converted strangers into friends and friends into? Ahhh, read on!

We stayed in touch regularly on phone, mobile, exchanging emails etc. I was in Mumbai and he in Delhi. Our friendship grew deep with each passing day.

In 2014, he moved to my city, Mumbai, and plunged to take the first step to meet me. I selected a noisy public place just to make things certain and play safe; I chose Hard Rock Café, which was certainly the worst selection!

At our first rendezvous, he was not a great conversationalist in person. I caught him several times stealing glances at me from the corner of his eyes, as if trying to drink in the most of me. I kept doing most of the gabbing. Yes, he was handsome and an avid listener!

Following Sunday, he invited me to his apartment in Juhu for a brunch. He had a great place overlooking the ocean and had prepared my favorite Italian cuisine. He served it with South

African reserve merlot. I really fancied men who could cook, I must add it was a turn on.

Some amazing retro tunes were playing on his Bang & Olufsen music system. After the meal, he held out his hand for a dance, and peculiarly, I was acting coy for the first time in my life, flushed like a little girl, so unlike the typical tomboy me.

We danced our first waltz to Engelbart Humperdinck's *Last Waltz Together*, bizarrely an ironical song for our first tango!

I laid my head on his shoulder as we lost count of time. Then I felt his hand reach for the nape of my neck, as his lips found mine. His kisses were passionate, craving for me, to devour my whole being.

I shut my eyes and extended my hand. He drew me close.

"Oh, my lord, you are perfect," escaped his lips.

With one swift move, he scooped me in his arms and carried my lithe frame to his bedroom up the flight of stairs.

We had forgotten time, lunch, wine as hours had passed and evening fell. He slipped his arm around my nimble frame and said, "Stay here tonight." This is what I had longed to hear forever. I cuddled with him and fell into a lull slumber, deeply satisfied and content as I felt his eyes looking at me lovingly, not letting me escape from his embrace.

Affection like this from a man was rare for me, and I intended to relish every moment of it. Having found each other, we decided not to lose this relationship. This was said in so many unsaid words. Love had arrived.

Epilogue

Many people reading the book might feel that I have stories of disasters all through, but let me assure you, all these experiences and my spiritual appetite, have carved a beautiful person out of me. Not at all resentful towards men, forgiving, ever giving love and not expecting in return, focused on my dreams, a bundle of positive energy bouncing all around. A magician who manifests everything and anything she wants, with the power of just her thoughts. In fact, all these bitter sweet experiences churned out a more patient loving empowered, unstoppable me! Thankyou Life. I release this book as I commence my fiftieth year!

This is my maiden venture at penning a book. So, ten out of the twelve narratives are true. I hope you relished the read. Do refer to friends if you did. Thankyou.

Sushma Seth and Vanndana Vaadera at a show

Vanndana Vaadera and PM of Sweden at the first Guwahati International Film Festival

Actor Rajneesh Duggal and Vanndana Vaadera judging a Wizcraft event